A Gift For

Olivia

From

Grandma Rachel

Merry Christmas
2020

Design and layout © 2012 Porch Swing Press, Nashville, Tennessee
Production Manager: Mike Stevens, Eveready Press, Nashville, Tennessee
Designer: S.P. Terrano, Yellowhouse, Inc., Franklin, Tennessee, www.yellowhouse.com

ISBN: 978-1-59530-708-8
BOK2166

Made in China
0819

WiseDogs™

H. Jackson Brown, Jr. • Dale C. Spartas

WORTHY
PUBLISHING
Brentwood, Tennessee

Dedication

To the dogs we have known and loved:

Poochie, Champ, Pedro, Tippy, Skip, Daisy, Abe, Eli, Jenny Lake, Clementine, Casey, Addy, Blue, Buck, Bud, Chip, Dumplin, Jessi, Magic, Meg, Pepper, Peppi, Purdey, Rose, Ruby and Spotty.

And to the dogs we wish we knew:

Dickens, Dottie, Tuna, Long John, Hot Ticket, Hoover, Tucker, Bob, Sassafras, Scout, Hazel, Otis, Boomer, BeBop, Smokey, Honey Bear, Tar Heel, Choo-Choo, DueBill, Wiggles, Wrigley, Razza, Romeo, Cheeseburger, Emily, Garbo, Gerty, Salsa, Gladstone, Winston, Party Girl, Gumdrop, Sammy, BowTie, Ivy, Mai Tai, Marley, Scooter, Leo, Skinner, Soot, Zelda, Sadie, Sarge, Tomba, Shadow, Sasha, Snookums, Rokie, Skeddaddle, Tutu, Tinker, Peanut, Spanky, Star, Sumo, Tasha, Stubby, Tubby, Cricket, Zeek, Woodstock, ZoomZoom, Yellowstone, Inca, Yukon, Spooky, Yanker, Roll-On, Mozart, Sydney, Psycho, Preacher, Rickytick, Rider, Daddy-O, Boo Boo, Hic-Up, Puddles, Rodeo, High Note, Babe, Twidder, Bear, Traveler, Sparky, Bon Bon, Gretta, Bulah, Nigel, Cleo, Zoe, Top Hat, Cool Whip, Cowboy, Nacho, Dude, Noodles, Doo Bee, Sacha, Time Out, Pot Luck, Zipper, Pizza Boy, Flag, Hawk, Bridger, Chap, Bud, Blue, Whistler, Drake, Widgeon, Smoke, Chance, Hailey, Howdy, Sam, Surge, Cornell, Nika, Rocket, Ripley, Ava, Dash, Fetchit, Nora, Nomad, Bozeman, Picasso, Paddy, Pearl, Domo, Dakota, Ginger, Omar, Ollie, Cheyene, Rooney, Reno, Tinker, Toby, Rufus, Lucy Blue, Nora, Chappy, Martini, Petey, Rondo, Lilly, Taco, Buster, Winsor, Raider, Ringer, Dixie, Woo Woo, Hawkeye, Rusty, Bogey, Sailor, Sunny, Coot, Tank, Shasta, Jazz, Mack, Loddy, Laddie, Lucky, Opal, Mick, Maggie, Allie, Iris, Rowdy, Chief, Chet, Miller, Dumpster, Wags, Ceasar, Spur, Turbo, Zoro, Barkley, Webster, Bella, Hitchcock, Cassidy, Breeze, Lucy, Chewey, Abbey, Abiline, Napa, Banjo, Biscuit, Topper, Winnie, Snowball, Waldo, Gretchen, Fridge, Holly, Molly, Riley and Smiley.

Photographer's Introduction

Dogs have always been a significant and meaningful part of my life. Often as I work I have a four-legged companion (or two) by my side, or sleeping at my feet, or nudging my hand, telling me "finish up; it's time for play!".

Since boyhood I have been drawn to dogs as they are to me. They grow from chubby, silly, little puppies into attentive, loving companions, and then into gray-muzzled senior citizens. I've trained many dogs, but the most important lessons learned were the ones I've actually been taught by the wonderful dogs who have passed through my life.

I am blessed and grateful for my family and friends, for my career, for a home on the river, and, of course, for all the wise dogs who have been in my life.

Dale C. Spartas
Big Sky Country, Montana

Author's Introduction

After my Life's Little Instruction Book® series became popular, I searched for a simple and convincing way to illustrate instructions from the books.

The answer became obvious when I met Dale Spartas and had the pleasure of viewing thousands of his superb photographs of sporting dogs. Something magical seemed to happen when a particular photo was matched with the appropriate instruction. His photographs communicated perfectly the characteristics of loyalty, discipline, purpose and courage that I had written about.

A quick glimpse of these pages confirms what we already know about our faithful companions; that the mystery behind their eyes and steadfastness of their spirit reveal noble hearts that have much to teach. May this book add proof to that.

So relax and let your imagination run free over these words and images. Then go find a dog and pet it. You might also want to add an encouraging, "Good dog. Good dog."

H. Jackson Brown, Jr.
Oak Hill, Tennessee

He seemed neither old nor young.
His strength lay in his eyes.
They look as old as the hills,
*   and as young and as wild.*
I never tired of looking into them.

— John Muir, about his dog Strickeen

My dog is so smart.
He thinks I'm a genius.

— H. Jackson Brown, Jr.

I could never bring myself
to think too highly of anyone
who didn't like my dog.

— H. Jackson Brown, Jr.

When you
feel great,
notify
your face.

Don't live
with the
brakes on.

Resist
snacking
between
meals.

Stop and read community bulletin boards.

Compliment
three people
every day.

Take a
chance.

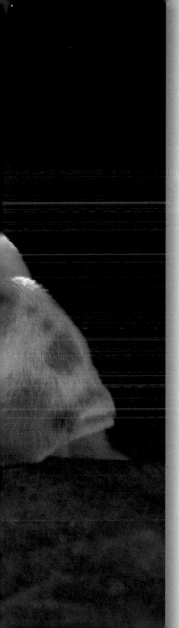

Remember
that the things
around you
are never as
important as
whose arms
are around you.

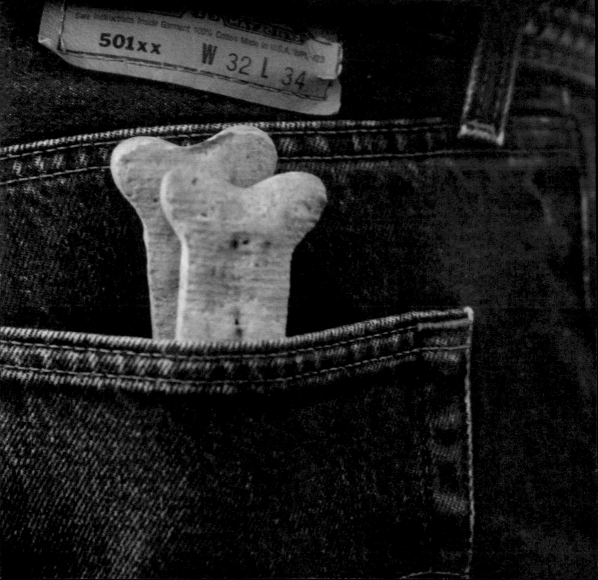

Be quick
to reward
good
behavior.

If someone
offers you a
breath mint,
take it.

Remember, consequences follow every decision.

Don't
skip breakfast.

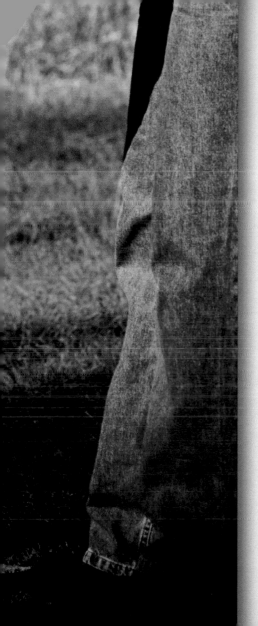

Be the first to say hello.

Resist temptation.

Stay informed of business trends.

Don't whine.

Retain
your dignity
regardless
of the
circumstances.

Have
a friend
who owns
a pick-up.

Don't
let a little
dispute
injure
a great
friendship.

Respect your elders.

Remember, love changes everything.

Keep your eye on the ball.

If you're going to sing, sing out loud.

When
something is unclear,
don't be afraid
to ask a question.

Know when to let someone else drive.

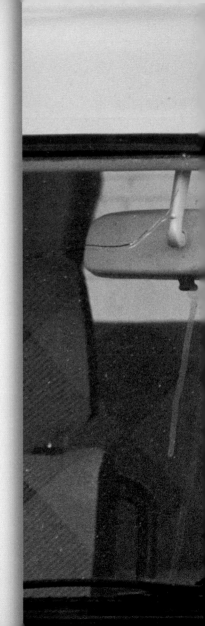

Practice patience.

Life will sometimes hand you a magical moment.

Savor it.

Be there when people need you.

When you're wrong, admit it.

Promise
big.

Deliver
big.

Don't hurry past beauty.

Never deprive someone of hope.

It may be all they have.

Watch
a sunrise
with someone
you love.

Be
the first to
volunteer.

Don't
pick up after
your children.

That's
their job.

Do small tasks well.

Know
when to leave
the office
party.

Remember,
you never lose
brain cells
by listening.

Win
with humility.

Lose
with dignity.

When you find
a job you love,
give it everything
you've got.

Remember,
everyone needs
a hand to hold
and a heart
to understand.

Good things are best when shared.

Never apologize for looking your best.

Remember,
anyone
can have
a bad day.

Waste time
with someone
you love.

Attend
class reunions.

Stand out
from
the crowd.

Remember, some things are worth waiting for.

When
you're
headed for
trouble,
take along
a friend.

Be home
for the holidays.

Take a
walk with
someone
you love
on a snowy
afternoon.

Never apologize for being early.

Silence.

Sometimes it's the best response.

When you're uncertain of what to do, follow the instructions.

To make a memory,
get muddy.

Believe
in love
at first sight.

Let the hard times make you stronger.

Remember,
who you're with
is always
more important
than where
you are.

When singing
the National Anthem,
remove your hat.

Be the one
who's not
afraid to shake
things up.

Remember, sometimes you'll have to hold your nose, close your eyes, and jump off the high board.

Time alone
is often
time well spent.

Avoid tight places and too-tight underwear.

Don't go
looking
for trouble.

Remember,
that winners
do what
losers don't
want to do.

Stand by your friends.

Protect and defend
those you love.

May your
dreams
defy the
laws of
gravity.

And remember,
your character
is your destiny.

If you have enjoyed this book
or it has touched your life in some way,
we would love to hear from you.

Please send your comments to:
Hallmark Book Feedback
P.O. Box 419034
Mail Drop 100
Kansas City, MO 64141

Or e-mail us at:
booknotes@hallmark.com